This book is dedicated to Krisana and Kyler. My inspiration, my pride, my silly monkeys, my beautiful children. May I too be your inspiration and pride because I will always be your silly mommy.
-M.K.

Copyright © 2020 by Marcela Klinsrisuk
Illustrations by Alejandra Lopez

All rights reserved. No part of this book may be reproduced or used in any manner whatsoever without the prior written permission of the author except for the use of brief quotations in a book review and certain other non-commercial uses permitted by copyright law.

This is a work of fiction. Names, characters, and incidents are either the products of the author's imagination or used in a fictitious manner. Any resemblance to actual persons or actual events is purely coincidental.

Published by Lion and Archer Books, New York
lionandarcherbooks@gmail.com
ISBN 978-1-7355948-4-2 (Paperback)
ISBN 978-1-7355948-5-9 (Hardcover)

My Friends from A to Z
A Fun Way to Learn the Alphabet

Marcela Klinsrisuk
illustrated by Alejandra López

Ana eats an apple

Brandon rides his bicycle

Camila naps with her cat

Daniel walks his **d**og

Ellie bathes an elephant

Fabian catches a frog

Gabriella plays her guitar

Henry wears his hat

Isabella looks at insects

Jonathan likes jam

Kayla flies her kite

Leo has a toy lion

Monica hugs her Mommy

Noah pretends to be a ninja

Olivia runs Outside

Patrick practices on the piano

Quinny saves quarters

Raymond splashes in the rain

Sandra dances and sings

Todd feeds his turtle

Ummi twirls her Umbrella

Victor loves his Veggies

Willow drinks a cup of Water

Xander taps his Xylophone

Yana stretches for Yoga

Alphabet

Aa  apple	Bb  bicycle	Cc  cat	Dd  dog	Ee  elephant
Ff  frog	Gg  guitar	Hh  hat	Ii  insects	Jj  jam
Kk  kite	Ll  lion	Mm  mommy	Nn  ninja	Oo  outside
Pp  piano	Qq  quarters	Rr  rain	Ss  sings	Tt  turtle
Uu  umbrella	Vv  veggies	Ww  water	Xx  xylophone	Yy  yoga
Zz  zoo				

www.ingramcontent.com/pod-product-compliance
Lightning Source LLC
Chambersburg PA
CBHW040509110526
44587CB00047B/4390